My Spiritual Unfolding: Science of Mind

By Rose Bruce, EdD, PhD

"The I AM works through us
to will and to do that which ought to be done by us."
Emma Curtis Hopkins

Maple Leaf Publishing Inc.
Alberta Canada

My Spiritual Unfolding
Copyright © 2020 by Rose B.

All rights reserved. No part of this book may be reproduced or transmitted in any form or by any means, electronic or mechanical, including photocopying, recording, or by any information storage and retrieval system, without written permission of the publisher.

ISBN Paperback: 978-1-77419-044-9
ISBN eBook: 978-1-77419-043-2
Rev. Date: June 8, 2020

MAPLE LEAF PUBLISHING INC.

3rd Floor 4915 54 St Red Deer,
Alberta T4N 2G7 Canada

General Inquiries & Customer Service
Phone: 1-(403)-356-0255
Toll Free: 1-(888)-498-9380
Email: info@mapleleafpublishinginc.com

Dedication

I would like to thank all of my teachers at The Center for Spiritual Living who gave tirelessly to me and the other students in the classes I took there: Reverend Edward Viljoen, Reverend Joyce Duffala, Elias Owens, and Reverend Ruth Barnhart. My understanding of Science of Mind grew gradually under the insight and nurturance of these wonderful people. I feel truly blessed.

This book is also dedicated to all those who are interested in Science of Mind and a spiritual life. It is a rich topic with many wonderful authors to read. This book mentions a few of them. Blessings to you on your road to spiritual understanding and insight.

Namaste, Rose

Foreword

A life well-lived balances both action and reflection. Action is obviously necessary to get things done. Reflection allows us to thoughtfully consider what we are about to do, and to learn from and improve upon what we have just done. Reflection ensures that our actions will be for the highest ethical good for as many people as possible, including ourselves.

You no doubt can think of ready examples of people you know—either personally or by public repute—who seem to jump into action without much reflection. Perhaps, like me, you may have made this mistake yourself at some time. I think we can agree that the results of too much action and not enough reflection are not optimal, and can even be disastrous.

What follows this foreword are the writings of a woman who has become quite masterful in the art of reflection, Dr. Rose Bruce. In this book, she reflects on previous life experiences, daily activities, and her new-found study of the work of 20th Century religious philosopher, Ernest Holmes, relating them all to her own spiritual philosophy of life.

I first met Rose Bruce in January 2019, when I was teaching a class at the Center for Spiritual Living, Santa Rosa entitled "Basic Principles of Science of Mind." This class is an introduction to Holmes's spiritual philosophy, and draws spiritual explorers from a diverse range of background and experience.

It quickly became obvious that Rose was a woman of rich experience and study, as evidenced by her thought-provoking questions, wisdom-filled statements, and committed drive to explore the material. It came as no surprise, then, when I found out Rose held two doctorates, and was a published author.

Touching again on the value of reflection, not only does it inform our actions, reflection is also a key element when we are learning a new body of knowledge. Reflection moves us from "I understand this intellectually" to "I personally find meaning in this for my own life." I am grateful that Rose continues to find personal meaning in her expanding understanding of Science of Mind, and has so generously offered us the wisdom gleaned from her reflections on this philosophy in the context of her very rich and thoughtful life.

Joyce Duffala, Ed.D
Assistant Minister,
Center for Spiritual Living, Santa Rosa
April, 2020

Contents

Dedication..1
Foreword...2-3
The Beginning...6
Surrender..7
Gratitude...8-9
Living in the Presence..10
Doubt...11
Being of Service...12
The Center for Spiritual Living...13
Old Thought vs. New Thought..14-15
Spirit, Mind, Body..16
Healing...17
Spiritual Mind Treatment...18-19
Projections...20
Seed Thought..21-22
Women's Retreat...23-24
Guided Meditation in the Redwood Glen................................25
A Spirit Walk..26
Four Swans Flying..27
A Near Fatal Car Crash..28-29
Response Paper on Thomas Troward..................................30-31
Our Bloated Nothingness..32
Becky..33-34-35

Still Fires	36-37
Spiritual Guidance and Discernment	38-39
Mental Practice	40
Spiritual Roots of Science of Mind	41-42
Thanksgiving	43
A Dinner Party	44
A Christmas Tree	45-46
A Tree Fell	47-48
A Dream	49-50
The Dinner Party	51-52
Christmas	53-54
My Support System	55-56
The New Year	57-58
Divine Love	59
Spiritual Mind Treatment To Release Worry	60-61
Spiritual Mind Treatment for Forgiveness	62
Moss and Ferns	63-64
Thursdays	65-66
Spiritual Mind Treatment	67-68
Spiritual Mind Treatment for Rose	69
What is Spiritual Mind Treatment?	70-71-72
Show Me The Way	73

The Beginning

I was reborn spiritually on July, 7, 2017 at the age of 67. Upon writing this I am struck by how many sevens there are. Seven is the number of completion or fulfillment. On that date I was spiritually broken. I was in my living room with my soon to be husband, Eric, and a neighbor, Amy. I was terribly upset, knew that there was something wrong with my life, had high blood pressure, and was at the end of my rope. I was retired and my life partner and wife of 20 years had passed on December 27, 2014. I was in deep grief and everything that had meaning in my life before was meaningless. I was also abusing alcohol. I said "I need help!" I had never said that in my life before. I now realize that not only did Eric and Amy, the Emergency Room staff, and the Intake Counselor hear me, but my Higher Power also heard me. I was finally able to totally surrender my will and my life over to a Higher Power I had forgotten a long time ago. Although I was raised Christian and had given my life over to Jesus at twelve years old, I had forgotten that pledge many years before and had been living on self-will for 67 years. I was ready to learn a new way of life.

My spiritual rebirth from that day until today has sometimes been sudden and at most times gradual. This book reflects some of my thoughts from recovery and from the past eighteen months studying and attending The Center for Spiritual Living in Santa Rosa, California. This Center is based on the teaching of Ernest Holmes called Science of Mind.

Surrender

Surrender is that moment when we realize and acknowledge to our innermost selves that we cannot stop drinking, that the option to "not drink" has been removed, that will power and desire to stop drinking have no effect to change our behavior. We may use different internal and external words like "I need help" or "I cannot do this anymore" or "I'm through living in this hell." Before surrender, our life is one of attempts to manage and control our drinking and everything else in our life. These efforts are futile. But it may take us many years to realize the reality of that statement. Negative consequences are usually rationalized away or ignored so that we can shift our attention to our "go to," to alcohol. Alcohol seems to be the answer to every situation in our lives: anxiety, sadness, relief, joy, celebration, feeling down… The mental preoccupation with alcohol can only be understood by an alcoholic. In the back of one's mind is always the thought "do I have enough alcohol on hand for today" or "when can I take my next drink" or "I need more." Life seems to be lived in a hurry to get to the reward, to "get to the next drink." I'm sure you know what I'm talking about.

Surrender is our moment of release from the powerful hold alcohol has on us. It is a moment of sanity and humility: we realize we do not have the answer to our lives, that our best efforts have left us broken, ashamed, humiliated, and defeated. Yet it is exactly in this moment that we are released and begin to feel the freedom from alcohol. We begin to learn how to live a completely new life. We "let go" and "let God."

Gradually surrender becomes a daily practice. Many of us start the day with the Third Step Prayer, I offer myself to Thee, to build with me and to do with me as Thou wilt… We learn to pause when agitated; to stop our automatic response to a situation, relax, and find our soul's integrity.

We look for opportunities to serve others. Our life has a new meaning. This is the gift of sobriety.

Gratitude

Gratitude for me is a matter of perception. It usually requires that I shift the kaleidoscope of my perception a few degrees away from my normal gaze and onto one of more light, beauty, and love. Often this shift is thrust upon me like when I am driving North up Highway 1 and I turn a curve in the road revealing a breathtaking view of the expanse of the Pacific Ocean with rocks and waves below the cliffs. Or when I suddenly glance up and see the blue sky above with soft white clouds drifting by.

I find myself grateful for nature

> A soft yellow duckling in the Spring
> Hearing the wind blowing through the trees
> A bee landing upon a flower
> The hooting of a barn owl in my backyard at night.

I find myself grateful for people in my life

> Friends who greet me at recovery meeting
> The safety and comfort I feel snuggled in bed next to my beloved
>
> Looking into the loving eyes of my sponsor
> Meeting a new sponsee and seeing the wonder and hope in their eyes.
>
> I am grateful for physical health
> For being able to walk five miles every day
> For waking up sober and turning my life over to a Higher
> For being able to see, hear, smell, and touch
> For feeling the strength in my legs.

But most of all I am grateful for the gift of sobriety for without it I would not be experiencing any of the things listed above. I would be lost in a prison of my own making yet not knowing any way out. I remember my last drunk and am humbled to my knees at the incredible transformation that has occurred in my life since walking into the rooms of recovery. A new way of living full of grace and opportunity has emerged out of the darkness. All that was required was surrender and trust.

Living in the Presence

In recovery we learn to live in what is referred to as the fourth dimension. This is a powerful shift in consciousness. When I came into recovery I was full of fear. The past was over, the present included profound grief over the loss of my wife of 20 years, and the future was bleak. I was lost in fear and had sought solace in alcohol. That lead me to deeper despair and suicidal attempts. I was confused and did not understand what was happening to me.

From the first moment I walked into the rooms of recovery I knew I was powerless over alcohol and that my life had become unmanageable. Being raised Lutheran it was easy for me to believe in a Power greater than myself including all of my new friends as well as a Creative Loving Energy I had turned away from years earlier. I trusted the group and the process.

With each meeting, each exchange with another person in recovery, every new day in sobriety, I learned to let go of the past, quit anticipating the future, and experience the NOW, the present moment. And the more I did that, prayed and meditated, I became aware of the PRESENCE which is an experience of the Diving unfolding in every person and situation. A new-found peace began to emerge and lasted longer and longer each day.

Today I practice the PRESENCE , that is, I constantly try to have my focus be on the wholeness and beauty of each moment. I remind myself, when I get anxious, that I have everything I need AT THIS MOMENT . Nothing more is required for me to feel peace and serenity...just to let go and BE IN THE MOMENT. This is much more than relief from alcohol, it is a profound new way of living that I am learning and practicing in each moment. How blessed I am!

Doubt

There are times when I lose my grip on life. Some unexpected news shatters my normal equanimity: a sudden need for surgery for a loved one, financial set back, someone close to me is dishonest... I find myself caught up in fear. I struggle to make sense of it all. I lose my perspective that things are unfolding as they should according to a plan beyond my comprehension. I lose my faith.

At these times I reach out to familiar coping mechanisms. I go to a meeting. I call my sponsor. I pray and meditate. I go back to basics: I am an alcoholic, my life is unmanageable at this moment, I need to turn my will and my life over to a power greater than myself.

Still I may stay in these uncomfortable feelings for days. I long for each day to be over as each minute seems like a struggle to find serenity and I just want to close my eyes and wake up to a new day. I put one step in front of the other and do not pick up a drink because I remember my last bottom and do not want to go through that again. Alcohol is not an answer for a reprieve.

The past few days have been like that. I'm in a learning phase. Today I went for a two hour walk with my sponsor. Walking around Spring Lake in the rain was wonderful. There were few people there and we could talk and share. She reminded me of the basics, we worked through a current resentment which was causing my mental upheaval. But beyond the techniques and suggestions, I felt her love. She didn't have to have all the answers for me, I just needed to feel that I was not alone, that someone cared, that I fit into the pattern of life. I needed to pause and feel the comfort of grace that is always available but that I had forgotten. The peace of the walk, the loving guidance, and the grace of the moment healed my fears and reminded me that I am a part of the unfolding mystery around me. We are each an essential part of the whole. That is why we are here. We matter.

Being of Service

Being of Service is a way of life in recovery. It is suggested, soon upon entering the rooms of recovery, that we take on a service commitment, usually making coffee. This is a wonderful way to get to know other people in recovery. You need to arrive early, take out the necessary equipment, put on the coffee, and wait for others to arrive. It feels a little awkward at first, not knowing anyone, but gradually you get to know people as they arrive and come over to help themselves to coffee and chat with you in a friendly sort of way. It feels good to be contributing to others, to be of service.

When I first started attending recovery meetings I went to six meetings a week and had three service commitments. I tried coffee, literature, and gradually took on "secretary" or the person who runs the meetings. I felt honored that others wanted me to contribute in these ways. I got used to being in front of the crown talking. I even got a little rowdy toward the end of my secretary commitment ready to try new things, to shake things up a little. Soon I found myself knowing just about everybody's name. I was a part of recovery.

That service has continued to grow. And I now realize that I had begun to shift my focus away from selfish things and onto my fellows. We can only focus on one thing at a time. If we are paying attention to others, we are not paying attention to ourselves. Our world expands to include others.

Perhaps the most wonderful thing we can experience is taking another through the recovery process, through the steps, is seeing the light come on in their eyes. Love and service, that is what recovery means to me. And with that comes freedom from myself and a life of purpose beyond what I could ever have imagined. One step at a time, one day at a time, my life has grown to include many new friends and loved ones. I feel an integral part of bringing recovery to the world. What better activity is there?

The Center for Spiritual Living

In December 2018 I was year and a half into sobriety and feeling a deep spiritual pull to go deeper in my connection with the Divine. Recovery had opened my heart to a Higher Power and my life was transforming according to God's will, not mine. I was experiencing moments of awareness of the Divine in my life, unfolding in the moment with everyone and everything that I saw around me. I was talking to a friend in recovery and he suggested that I try the Center for Spiritual Living located in our city. I thought about it but did not act upon it. Then another person in recovery said the same thing to me, but I ignored it again (obviously not following the Divine Guidance I was receiving). Finally, in early January I was having breakfast alone at my favorite local coffee shop reading The Sermon and the Mount by Emmet Fox when the man at the table next to me asked if I was enjoying my book. I said I was and he said "if you like that, you might try the Center for Spiritual Living." I finally heard the guidance and decided to go that next week.

I looked up the Center on the web and saw that there was a free discussion on the principles of the Center on Wednesday evenings. I went to that meeting. It was an introduction to the Science of Mind as taught by Ernest Holmest which serves as the basis for their teachings and work. There was much that I did not understand, however, I was able to express that "I felt the Divine all around me and wanted to know how to handle that energy. Was I in the right place?" They assured me that I was and I felt reassured.

Sunday I went to the regular service and was inspired the service and a sermon by Reverend Edward Viljoen. I went again the next Wednesday and learned that they were starting classes on understanding the teaching of the Center. I signed up for one to begin the next week: a ten-week class on the Basic Concepts of Science of Mind. I was excited and felt I was on the right track.

Old Thought vs. New Thought

I am in my first class called Basic Principles of the Science of Mind. I am excited to be embarking on a new field of study. The first class was spent discussing the difference between Old Thought and New Thought in terms of a religions understanding. Old theology taught ideas of good and evil, it was fear based, Divinity was perceived of as being outside ourselves, arbitrary, and there were strict rules regarding our thoughts and behaviors. New Though is characterized by the concept of one power that is love-based, the idea that we are evolving to a higher Good, we are one with Divinity, our thoughts are creative and we are perfect and whole. We then spent time listing all of the names of God that we could recall.

There are two phases of mind: surface mind which is our consciousness and deep mind which is our unconscious or subconscious mind. Our thoughts are creative. They move from consciousness to deeper mind which then prompts the manifestations of our life. The central idea is that the Universe says "yes" to our thoughts. Therefore, our life represents our thoughts, conscious and unconscious. It is analogous to a loom on which a weaver weaves cloth. The Universe is the loom and our thoughts are creating the cloth of our experiences. Hence it is very important to explore and bring to consciousness thoughts which we absorbed from our family and society which govern our lives, even though we don't know it. The creation of our life through conscious and unconscious thoughts is called the Law of Cause and Effect. The task in life is to become more conscious of our thoughts which are habitual and constant. A change in our thoughts will lead to a change in life circumstances.

Material thinking is focused on what is outside of us. Spiritual thinking is focused on what is happening inside us; our connection to God. In Science of Mind we turn away from external circumstances and focus on the internal mind state that we wish to manifest in our lives. We learn to do Spiritual Mind Treatment, which is a method of shifting our focus from the causes of suffering in our life to the qualities of God that replace this error in consciousness.

Qualities of God, the Divine Essence, include peace, serenity, loving kindness, harmony, power, beauty, wisdom, and so forth.

The first step in building a consciousness of our true worth is letting go of negative thinking. We do not get caught in self-blame for our problems and suffering in our past, we see the past as a learning process. We shift our focus to positive statements. This is more than positive thinking and affirmations. It is a radical shift in consciousness from error to Truth. Power flows from the focus of our attention. So, we start with moving our attention to positive, uplifting statements about ourselves and others. We then attract to us what we have focused on which is the Law of Attraction. We let go of negative attitudes because hostility, judgments, and resentments toward others bock the flow of Divine creativity. The attitude we must take toward those who have hurt us is forgiveness.

The practical application of these principles can be experienced by (1) listing the desired conditions for your life and (2) listing the qualities that the River of Perfect Mind will manifest in your life. For example: I have a desired condition of sobriety, love shared between me and my husband, physical health and daily exercise, meaningful work, and prosperity. The qualities I want manifested in my life are love, joy, peace, abundance, and physical healing. The affirmations need to be in the present tense ("I am...") and affirmative ("I am..." vs "I am not..."). They need to be believable to you at this time.

I was participating fully in the class activities. However, a part of me was holding back thinking: this is someone else's conclusions about how the Universe works. I'm not sure it is mine. What I was aware of was that I could sense Divine energy in me and others and in between us. I also sensed that most people were blocking this energy. I wanted to learn how to direct the energy in a positive way for myself and other people. I did feel that this teaching might help me learn how to do that.

Spirit, Mind, Body

One of the central concepts that we were taught was that God is composed of Spirit, Mind and Body. We similarly are composed of spirit, mind, and body. This was taught by drawing two circles. In the one on the left, the three aspects of God were listed. On the right were the concepts of humans presented. We were asked to draw this in our notebooks while the instructor Reverend Joyce Duffala walked around to check on our progress. Well when I was thinking about this during our reading before class, it seemed to me that rather than having two circles, I ought to draw one circle with a perpendicular line down the middle dividing into two equal parts on each side. Then each side had two parallel lines separating the Spirit (spirit), Mind (mind), and Body (body). I thought it was obvious: if God was everything why would there be a separate circle? When Joyce saw my figure she said "this is brilliant". I was flattered and encouraged.

Healing

The Body of God is the Universe. The body of humans is our life, body, all that which is manifest in our lives. The great significance in healing is the fact that our physical body is characterized by inertia: it stays going in the direction it is headed. If it is still, it stays still. If it is moving in a certain direction, it stays moving in that direction. The creator of the body is our thoughts. In Science of Mind we say there are no incurable diseases because there is no limit to our acceptance of the truth of our wholeness. When results are not forthcoming when we think they should be, we should constantly shift of our awareness to the thoughts of what we want to create in our lives. Healing is a shift in consciousness. There is in fact nothings to heal. We are naturally whole, healthy and complete. However, we have forgotten that.

What I am getting from our instructor Joyce is a sense of validation for who I am. I am also receiving the gift of paying attention to others and what their needs and wants are.

We did an exercise today at the start of class that was very upsetting to me. The meditation was to remember being with someone or in a situation where we felt loved. I immediately thought of Leslie, my wife of twenty years who passed away four years ago, and tears began to roll down my face. I could not stop crying. Every time I tried to focus on what we were being taught, I was overwhelmed with grief. I finally asked one of the Practitioners in the class to help me. I went out with Tom. I told him what I was feeling and he comforted me saying "of course you are feeling this way. You ARE love and your love for Leslie is what you are experiencing." I felt a huge sigh of relief and relaxation. I just let that reality sink into my being. I was overcome again with emotion and this time it was joy, the joy of KNOWING I AM LOVE. The grief, where I was pushing away my love of Leslie because it hurt so much for her to be gone, was replaced by my moving INTO that love and finding relief. That feeling stayed with me for a long time.

Spiritual Mind Treatment

We are now studying Spiritual Mind Treatment, or a type of affirmative prayer that is used for healing. The foundation of authority is knowing. What bearing does this have on healing the physical body? When we know it is already done (the healing), it is accomplished. We are exploring the Law of Creation. We can manifest anything in Spirit/Mind. In Science of Mind we are encouraged to apply the principles we are learning to our own lives until we experience the reality of them. Then we know that they work. It is not an intellectual exercise. It is a matter of belief and then experience.

> "And suddenly you know, it's time to start something new and trust the magic of new beginnings." Meister Eckhart

There are five steps in a Spiritual Mind Treatment. In Spiritual Mind Treatment we are changing the consciousness of the Practitioner about the perceived condition in the Client. We align our consciousness to the Truth in which the condition does not exist. It is done in the NOW. And when it is done, it is finished and complete. We start by getting into a relaxed state of mind. The steps are:

1. Recognition of the truth of Spirit: that it is unconditional love, omnipresent, omnipotent, and omniscient.
2. Unification: that we are an individualized expression of the Divine, a part of Spirit, and so is the person we are treating for.
3. Realization: We realize that the condition is false and align with the truth of our being. We see the quality of the Divine that replaces the condition we see in our Client's life. God is light, life, joy, beauty, love, peace and power.
4. Thanksgiving: We give thanks for the reality of this truth.
5. Release: We acknowledge that it has already been changed in consciousness and will continue to unfold in our affairs as time moves forward.

I am now practicing using Spiritual Mind Treatment to deal with people and situations that are disturbing me. I find when I go through the steps, my mind is re-centered in the truth of life and shifted away from the disturbance of the lack that I am perceiving. I am finding more peace and serenity. I am finding a way to heal my consciousness.

Projections

Just came home from my class on the philosophical roots of Ernest Holmes and Science of Mind. We were discussing how our innermost assumptions about life keep being manifested in our lives until we can see and confront them once again. I said "well it sounds like we are just projecting onto the world." The instructor Rev. Ruth Barnhart said "Yes." "Then the logical consequence of that is that we will continue to remove our projections until we are finally faced with Truth which is Love. Then we will probably want to return and help others remove their projections," I said. "Yes, that is what all of the Master's have done" she replied.

Wow! I think I finally get it!

Another quote we discussed from Emerson is "Our faith comes in moments; our vice is habitual." (Emerson's Essays, p. 188). What this means to me is that we need to be constantly working on changing our assumptions about the world to see Truth and start recreating the reality that reflects these assumptions. Again, I see my life repeating patterns of relationships that reflect how I assume they should work. Right now, I am aware of a pattern of codependent reactions with Eric and we are now in counseling for me to try to understand my part in this and, of course, for him to understand his part in it. It's quite exciting. I don't feel a sense of blame but rather a sense of excitement about recognizing these patterns and changing them.

As they say in recovery and in Science of Mind: "How free do you want to be?"

I realize that I want to return to reading A Course in Miracles for in it Jesus talks about how we are projecting our perceptions onto the world.

I went for my walk to day and realized I am feeling uplifted by Spirit just like the birds I saw who were gracefully floating on the wind currents. I simply have to let go and let God.

Seed Thought

In class week, we were asked to conceive of a "seed thought" that we would like to see materialized by the end of the class or longer. What immediately came to mind for me was this book and its unfolding. We were to state what the "seed thought" was and then notice each day as evidence of Divine Guidance came to us from our lives.

I am amazed at how smoothly and consistently this book unfolding is happening. It is just like with my first book. It is almost writing itself. And each day I get a prompt from an email to go one step further with the process. This morning it was an email from the CEO of the film production company that is interested in possible doing a short documentary. He included specific instructions of what I need to do to qualify. I have most criteria but have a few to go including a screen play of my first book, a "Hollywood treatment", and "pitch materials." Fortunate, I was contacted by someone a few months ago offering to do just that. I told that person I would get back to them after the Canada book signing events. I sent that person an email saying I would like to proceed.

It is just like the first book; each day a little something happens that prompts me to believe that it is God's will for these materials to be released to the public. I know there is a great need in our culture for a contemporary female voice in recovery. I have certainly contributed in my own small way in shifting the trend of seeing women as subservient to men to people of their own right with the ability to work professionally, handling both family and job at the same time.

I am sure it is hard for women of today to even comprehend such archaic thinking as women not being able to have a career and home. But I lived through the 1950's where that was certainly the case. Women stayed home, took care of the children and their husband, and were subservient in every way. Thank God that has changed some.

Of course, I went on to earn two doctorates, probably to get back at the stereotypes I grew up with. I recall, when studying Martial Arts, of being so angry at these dictates and saying to myself "I'll prove you all wrong" which I did. Most people in my life thought I was off my rocker studying Martial Arts. "What do you need that for" they would say. Well as my Master's Thesis proved, I needed it to learn self-reliance and self-discipline. I LOVED throwing men on the mat. A new man would come into the dojo and want to learn the skills. I was usually paired with such a person. He would throw me into the mat as hard as he could, probably proving how macho he was. Well I would not say a word but would proceed to throw him just as hard as he had thrown me. He learned by that experience to be soft. Men learned to be soft and gentle and women learned to be self-reliant. That is what I found from administering The Meyes Briggs Type Inventory to male and female white belters and black belters. Women also showed a profile similar to female Olympic competitors as reflected in their scores on the Edwards Personal Preference Schedule. I was studying for my Masters Degree in Counseling at the time of my research on Martial Artists so it was easy to apply personality tests to my subjects. These results were presented at an annual meeting of JuJitsu participants.

Women's Retreat

I'm at my first Annual Recovery Women's Retreat in the redwoods in Northern California. I've never been around so many women at one time, around 150. I'm used to conferences that used to be dominated by men and I watch as women gradually were added to become equal in number to the men. This has a completely different feel. I am a little uncomfortable.

This is yoga time 7:00 – 8:00 a.m. But I am spoiled when it comes to studying yoga in the United States because I was instructed by a teacher from India, Pondurangadas. He used to be a Long Shoreman in New York. In the 1960's he left that job, moved to India, and came back a thin spiritual and yoga teacher.

I don't remember how I met him. He was living in Berkeley at the time in the 1970's. I invited him to come teach an all-day yoga workshop at the small town where I was going to college. He can and it was wonderful!

He taught that yoga is about "yoking" or "connecting to God." Pondurangadas taught that Yatha Yoga was about paying attention to the body; finding that point in your body in a pose where you have stretched as far as you can then exhaling into it which causes a natural relaxing of the body and stretching a little bit further. It was NOT about "getting into a stance"; it was about noticing the point of resistance and softening into it. I also think, now, that that was an analogy to paying attention to each moment's consciousness.

I've studied Hatha Yoga in the United States and have found it most disappointing. The instructors invariably focus on reaching a certain position. It has been Westernized into an external focus of achievement – so typical of our society. This misses the essential point.

One summer day in the 1970'2 I felt drawn to go to an outdoor festival at a city near where I was going to college. I was walking around by myself and I spotted Pondurangadas in the crowd. We walked toward each other and embraced. He pulled back and said "so you are why I am here. I was wondering why I was coming today." We strolled around together and he found for me a used copy of the Bhagavad Gita which I purchased and read.

Guided Meditation in the Redwood Glen

I just went for a group guided meditation in a grove of very old and majestic redwood trees. As I laid down to rest and hear the meditation, when I looked up, I was awestruck by the beauty above. The tops of the grove of trees made a canopy that was filled with light.

What caught my attention was a very tall redwood gently swaying in the wind. It gracefully rocked back and forth with the top one third of its majestic 750 feet trunk rocking repeatedly back and forth. When the meditation music started to play, I started to cry at the beauty of the moment. I borrowed a friend's cell phone to capture a picture of it at that perfect moment.

The meditation went on for a half hour but I was fixed on the pageantry above. I heard redwood needles drop occasionally and one pine cone fall. I was mesmerized.

A Spirit Walk

Tonight, we did a "spirit walk." It consisted of two lines of women facing each other and then each one of us took turns being blind folded and led down that line. Each woman in the line walked up to the woman in the middle, touched her shoulder, and spoke into their ear some positive statement about her.

The affirmation that hit my core was "Rose, you are good enough"or "Rose you are worthy." This hit my deep wound from childhood thinking I was "not good enough." I was never told this directly, rather the opposite. I was told I could do anything I set my mind to. But the feeling of "not good enough" somehow passed into my unconscious. It came from society at the time and probably from my family as well and generations before that. This is the message that has spurred me on my whole life to achieve difficult things like my Black Belt in Ju Jitsu and two doctorates. I figured a doctorate from the University of California Berkeley would finally allow me to speak my mind and be taken seriously. It certainly helped. But nothing could erase that subtle voice of doubt and uncertainty, that voice of unworthiness. I needed to learn to listen to and trust my inner wisdom, my intuition, which is what I am doing now.

I have tried hard to change this belief of unworthiness. It is finally melting away thanks all of the love and unconditional love I am receiving in recovery and from my spiritual unfolding. I have learned to trust my inner wisdom, my intuition. This is a feeling of "knowing" my truth, experiencing my truth and my connection with my Higher Power. I am now recognizing myself to be an Individualized Expression of the Divine, a unique manifestation of the Great Spirit. What a healing. What a blessing!

Four Swans Flying

On my walk this morning I was suddenly startled by the loud sound of four swans flying by me across the lake. They were very close and I could hear their wings going swish swish in the air loud and clear. It was breathtaking.

Recently I have come to the awareness that I am becoming a metaphysician. This is particularly touching to me as my early adult goal was to become a physician. As I have grown and experienced more in life, I have realized my interest is not so much in the body but in the mind and spirit. Being a Jungian Therapist was a goal in my 30's until the receptionist at the Jungian Institute in San Francisco told me I was too young and to come back when I was 50 years old. I was heartbroken and cried a lot that night.

But now I find myself studying metaphysics and feeling quite at home with it all. I've learned that the intellectual and spiritual movements of the early 20th century were influenced by such writer and thinkers as Ralph Waldo Emerson and Henry David Thoreau (the Transcendentalists), Bill W and Dr. Bob (of Alcoholics Anonymous), Carl Jung, William James, Ernest Holmes, Emma Curtis Hopkins, Aldous Huxley and other. This intellectual and spiritual zeitgeist of the time changed the thinking in the fields of metaphysics, religion, and psychology. Clearly the time was ripe for this new spiritual focus in Western Thought. They are all pointing to a similar source of knowledge and wisdom that we take so for granted today.

I feel so very thankful that my experience and understanding of this wisdom is readily available to me and continues to deepen.

A Near Fatal Car Crash

My husband and I like to take Thursday afternoon and evening to ourselves. We usually drive three hours North on Highway 1 which is a twisty narrow road with breathtaking scenery of the cliffs and ocean below. We are not in a hurry. I am quite familiar with the route and drive rather rapidly in my car. I love to turn up the radio and share my internal changes of late and to catch-up on Eric's latest thoughts and experiences. It is a time for us to reconnect.

This Thursday Eric's mom, who has alzheimer's, was with us. The power went out in her home, which in a county 1 1/2 hours North of us. Eric has driven up the night before to get her and have her stay with us for a few days.

We had driven up, had a wonderful dinner with an ocean view at a restaurant we frequented often. We were coming home. It was about 9:30 at night, dark, and I was joking about watching Steven Colbert. We were having a great time. There was a quick turn in the road, typical for that highway, when suddenly there were two bright lights coming right at us. I registered on it and thought "the car in in my lane. Is it swerving to pass another?" I blinked and registered that this was not the case. I thought "No it is coming straight at us. I guess I had better turn off on the right to avoid and accident." I pulled onto a wide shoulder area and the car drove toward us. It seemed to be accelerating. It passed so close we could hear the wind and our car shook. I thought it might hit my driver's side rearview mirror, but it didn't. I honked the horn for a long time. Then I started to shake. I called 911 and reported it.

The sighting of the car and the swerve took only three seconds. It was that fast. After we swerved out of the way and stopped by the side of the road, I felt a new sensation. I felt "held in God's hand." I realized and felt the fact that at each moment in my life I am held by God. If it is my time to go then it is my time to go. If it is my time to live, that is also by God's grace.

Becky, Eric and I talked for a brief time about the near-death car crash then we fell silent for a long time. We had been one second away from having a head-on collision. Had I not swerved, we would all now be dead...

About three months ago I had a dream of that exact scene. I was driving South on that narrow highway and a car suddenly appeared heading straight toward me. What I recall most vividly in my dream and in the actual incident is the brightness of the car's lights facing me. They bore into me relentlessly, not swerving at all but coming straight toward me. In my dream I turned abruptly right into some bushes. In reality I turned right into a short strip of shoulder just wide enough for our one car.

I feel that Divine Intelligence had prepared me for the event. In actuality that entire route is mostly narrow twisty turns with one foot at each side surrounded by tall redwoods. There are VERY FEW shoulders or turn-outs along the entire route. What a blessing that I responded the way I did! What blessing to be alive.

The scene keeps repeating in my mind over and over. That is the case for Eric and Becky also. We are stunned and extremely thankful to be alive! I realize it is not my time to go yet. It is just that simple. As Leslie said in her letter to me after her death "You have more to do...More to offer".

Response Paper on Thomas Troward

The idea I would like to discuss from The Edinburgh and Dore Lectures on Mental Science (chapters 12-16) is from chapter 15: The Soul.

> Intuition, the faculty of the soul, can be cultivated by meditating upon abstract principles related to a particular subject, and we can employ the imagination to convert intuitive perceptions to individual purposes. We find that intuition presents ideas from Universal Mind to the imagination in essence rather than definite form. The imagination then gives these ideas as clear and definite form relative to the individual purposes.

As I mentioned in class, I frequently receive intuitive hits when I am asleep either in dreams or ideas that are fresh in my mind when I wake up. When I go to sleep at night as I am reviewing the day, giving thanks for all of the wonderful things that have happened and seeing if I owe anyone an "amends," I end with the suggestion that my body is healing, returning to perfect original health. Then I say I am falling into a deep sleep and am open to guidance from the Divine through dreams or intuition.

When I awake if there is an idea or concept that pops into my consciousness, I pay attention to it. I figure out if there are some specific things I need to do, which often there are very specific actions I can take in my life to follow the guidance I have received. In this way I am tuning into the Divine a little bit more each day.

After reading the quote above I see that my habits before falling asleep are focusing on aspects of Divine Mind: namely health, guidance, and connection.

I have been amazed over the past year as I have studied Science of Mind and applying the concepts presented, how more focused my mind is upon the intention of aligning with Divine attributes. In January, during my first class, Core Concepts, I set the intention of selling books this year (a book I released in September 2018). Since that time, I have been contacted by a publisher, Maple Leaf Publishing, and practically every day I receive an email or phone call leading me in a new direction of social media postings of the book, book signings, and now translation rights into four languages and a short documentary film. I felt led to write the book, it was an accounting of my personal journal of ideas, thoughts, and experiences during my first nine months in recovery. Divine Principle has manifested a path far greater than anything I could have imagined. Whenever my self-will starts to take over, things fall apart and a greater plan reveals itself. It is awe inspiring.

Our Bloated Nothingness

I am at my husband's 30th High School Reunion. After three hours of meeting strangers I've reached my limit. The dinner is over and guests are getting loaded and loud as they dance to the music of a band. We are at a bar with a patio in the back for the crown of 300+ attendees to mingle.

I keep thinking about Ralph Waldo Emerson's "bloated nothingness" mentioned in his lectures. That is what I see around me: unconscious people caught up in their stories about themselves, their past activities and seeming importance.

I never did like bars. I never felt comfortable in them. The loud music prohibits any real conversation and the relating seems to be superficial. The Beatles imitation acoustic band here really had the crowd going. Guess it is a good night to "check out" of reality.

However, in sobriety there is no "checking out. Fortunately, I did not for a second feel like drinking. Thank God that compulsion has been lifted. However, I am present and aware and I'd rather be by myself in the car writing and reflecting than feeling isolated staring at strangers bounce around to the band. I am a true introvert.

Thank goodness I brought a meditation book from the Center for Spiritual Living. How refreshing to open it up and read. I already feel centered again. In it I read:

> This is a great reminder to not settle for the average and to be mindful of what the group mind asserts is normal. Especially in the spiritual realm where we are called to look higher, deeper and more clearly into the nature of things. So that we may remain unconvinced that chaos is inevitable or that ordinary is as high as we may aspire.
> (by Rev. Edward Viljoen)

How refreshing and just what I needed to feel sane and comfortable in my own skin again.

Becky

Today there are fires all around me in Northern California. I am writing by candle light.

I have not written about Becky, Eric's mom, very much lately. She has Alzheimer's. We go up to her home and hour and a half's drive both ways at least once a week to take care of her: fill her medication trays, buy groceries, do menus for the week, check on the caregiver's notes, et cetera. Almost every day we receive a call from the caregivers with questions or concerns. During the course of the last two year she has gradually gotten more and more afflicted by the disease.

Today she is North in the county where she lives. Yesterday both she and we had power outages. Now neither of us have power. Eric just left to try to get through on the one route out of five that is open to get to her home. She is out of pain medications today and we have the new fentanyl patches and hydromorphone pills for the month. We have no choice but to try to get them to her.

Becky's disease has progressed so that she now has very little short- term memory. When we take her out for a meal she will decide what she wants and by the time the waitress comes for her order, she will have forgotten it. We have to leave notes up on the walls reminding her to do things like "keep the blinds closed so it does not get too hot in the kitchen" or "do not answer the door at night" or "take your p.m. pill when the alarm goes off." Still we have to call and remind her to do these things.

She is forgetting where she lives now and gets confused when she goes out to have a cigarette. I bought her an identification. bracelet with her name, address, ALZHERIMER'S, plus our phone numbers on it. It helps her. It is time to get her into a home soon for her own safety.

She has caregivers who come each day from 1:00 pm until 6:00 p.m. They prepare meals, give her the medications, take her out to smoke cigarettes (her favorite thing) and socialize with neighbors, or to go to the movies. She wants to get everything she sees. If we go to the grocery store she will put items in the basket even though she has them at home. We have to take them out and people stare at us as though we are being mean to her. She will not remember when we get home what we bought. When we take her out for dinner she will not eat her meal and want desert. In short: she is now the child and we are the parents. This has been a subtle but consistent change especially for the last two years. Fortunately, she has a pleasant nature. Still it is trying to be around.

This is very difficult on my husband, Eric. We are doing all we can to help her but nothings will stop this disease from progressing. We feel helpless. We are now exploring options for 24 hours care which we cannot afford. Most likely she will end up in a care facility for people with memory problems which costs about $6,000 per month. We cannot afford this and she only has Social Security. So, we will need funding from the State. I am starting to look into how we can arrange for that.

As hard as we and the doctors try, she is slipping away. Our task now is to keep her safe. When Eric went up this time to get her she had invited a homeless drug addicted man into her home. This is totally unacceptable! She does not realize he might steal her meds and whatever else there is of value in her home, most of which caregivers have already stolen. She is just trying to help him.

Eric just left to try to reach her with her meds and I am a home writing by candle light. There is no way for him and I to talk because there is no internet for our phones to use. If he can he will try to send a text at some point to let me know how he is doing. Maybe I can go to the Starbuck's coffee shop that has internet tomorrow and charge my cell phone.

Becky will come and stay with us for a few days. This is challenging for Eric and me, but I've gotten more used to it. She likes to watch TV all of the time and smoke outside. I make sure she has lots of good food to eat and liquids to drink. We go out for brunch most days (when there is electricity). I give her the meds and a bath when we change the fentanyl patch.

Becky likes to take pretty things from our home. This is very typical of Alzheimer's patients. She will see a bracelet, ring, glass heart et cetera and put it into her purse or bag of clothes. We have talked to her asking her to not do this and it stops for a while, but it always comes back. We go through her things before we leave to take her home and pull out most of the things she grabbed. If I don't mind her having it, I let her take it home.

Thank goodness I am in recovery! I know I my heart and soul I am not alone. I am safe and held in unconditional love and support no matter what the external circumstances of my life may be.

The sun is setting. I pray for safety and comfort for all of the people affected by the fires. Over 200,000 people have been evacuated and most of Northern California, where we live, is without power. About 157 structures have burned and 57 of those were homes. I am blessed to be in my home tonight. God bless us all.

Still Fires

Day four of the fires in our area, Northern California. There are fires all around us. We can see the flames and smell the smoke. We live in Sonoma County in Northern California. It is an emergency situation. Still I feel calm. My sponsor texted me and I got in touch with my sponsees, such is the support and connection in recovery. We are all o.k. I misplaced my cell phone which was turned off so I am not sure how I will find it. Last night I was kept awake by some electrical devices calling out "low battery...low battery." I discovered this morning it is the hand held phone, which we have five of. So, I took out the batteries. They will recharge when we get electricity back.

There are 3,500 fire fighters battling the blaze. I found an emergency radio that Leslie bought years ago. I have had it sitting in my office window facing toward the sun to charge the solar batteries for years. It is my only source of information about what is going on. Over a million and a half people are displaced or without electricity. This may last two weeks.

I am keeping up with my routines: morning prayer and meditation and a five mile walk in the morning around the lake (with mask on of course). The air quality is very bad. I only saw a handful of people on my walk when normally there are a dozen or more.

We still have running hot water thanks to a generator on our neighborhood well and gas water heater. I just took a hot shower which felt great! I practically feel normal again.

I was able to buy ice and sandwich makings at the one grocery store in the area that is open so we will have plenty of food to eat. We have lots of bottled water as that is what we usually drink. We have a cooler to keep these few items cool. The refrigerator and freezers cannot be opened. Food can last for a few days. After that, it all has to be thrown out.

There is much to be thankful for. We are still home sleeping in our bed while most people are on cots in shelters. It is 72 degrees in the afternoons which heats up the house. However, it is getting nearly freezing at night and we cannot have a fire in the wood stove because of the poor air quality. So, we bundle up.

A neighbor called on me yesterday which was very reassuring. One neighbor has a home generator for their home, they have a baby to keep warm. I will buy one as soon as they are available again. I've had enough. The last great fire here was in 2017. It looks like it might be an annual event thanks to global warming.

I am enjoying this moment of peace. Fear is all around. Faith is the antidote.

God is my strength... God is my protection...
God is my strength... God is my protection...
God is my strength... God is my protection...
God is my strength... God is my protection...
God is my strength... God is my protection...
God is my strength... God is my protection...

Spiritual Guidance and Discernment

As I mentioned earlier, I go to bed asking for Divine Guidance. Lately what has been happening is that I have been receiving emails about my book from unexpected sources. One, in French, was from a film producer in France interested in doing a film about my book. I have had exchanges with him and we are moving forward on this project. Yesterday I received an email from someone about a radio interview. That felt right also so I moved ahead with it. Some emails do not feel right and I decline the offers that are coming regarding my first book. I believe that God is in charge of this project and it will unfold as it should if I just use discernment.

This can be very subtle. In the publishing industry I am finding there is an emphasis on ego. They want to appeal to my ego and to promote me, the author. I reemphasize that I am anonymous and that the book is not about me. The book is about the reality of a spiritual life available to all of us if we let go and give our life to the Divine. Some do not understand this and I refuse to deal with these people. The book is an act of service.

What I am trying to describe is the feeling that the book is unfolding as it should. God is in charge of this. And my job is to stay out of the way. I trust that I am being guided and receive much help in the classes that I am currently taking at the Center for Spiritual Living. They currently are discussing just this topic.

To stay centered I keep doing my familiar daily routines. The morning prayers and meditation center me. Then the two-hour walk around the lake brings me serenity. I love stopping at the same bench each day and seeing the same serene view of the lake, the reeds on the side, ducks and geese swimming by, and the hills reflected in the lake. How soothing it is that as my life changes there is stillness and steadiness at that bench. It is untouched by my affairs.

About two months ago I was saying I had no friends. I am noticing that now invitations are coming in for me to join a women's group, speak at a meeting, go for coffee... Clearly the universe has said "yes" to my desire to have close women friends in my life. I simply needed to be open to seeing the possibilities.

When I was reading The Sermon on the Mount by Emmet Fox about ten months ago, I was struck by a paragraph about "Give us this day our daily bread." Emmet Fox was expanding that this refers not only to the bread we eat, but to all that we need in life: friends, family, inspiration, books, finances, work, and so forth. He noted that our lives should be interesting. That struck me because at the time my life was not active and interesting enough for me. Now it is. I simply needed to open to and accept the invitations that were all around.

The sermon the week after the fires ended was about gratitude. How important it is to focus on gratitude especially when we are feeling overwhelmed by life's challenges. Some suggest doing a gratitude list daily for a month. The point is that as we notice things to be grateful for, we attract them to us. This is called the Law of Attraction. How important it is to pay attention to what we are thinking.

Scientific Christian: Mental Practice
By Emma Curtis Hopkins

This powerful book is life changing. It emphasis certain attitudes and practices that, if done consistently, will change the life of the Science of Mind Practitioner and touch those around them.

Here are a few quotes that have meaning to me:

> God is omnipotent, omnipresent, and omniscient.
> In God I live and move and have my being.
> The I AM works through me to will and to do that which ought to be done by me.
> Mind will demonstrate as much greatness as it has courage to stand by its intention.
> I am to keep the words of truth going within me continuously.
> I must give up guilt (belief in personal sin or wrongdoing) and blame (the belief in sin or wrongdoing of others).
> I must pronounce myself as a spiritual being with spiritual powers to heal.

Emma Curtis Hopkins speaks of a living, vibrant and personal experience of the Divine NOW. She reassuringly tells us we will be given the strength and guidance to do that which is ours to do. Our task is to constantly mind our thoughts to not accept any doubt or blame for ourselves or others. Then the Good within each of us will be manifest.

These are ideas to be savored and practiced throughout a whole lifetime. This is a goal to aspire to. It is a map toward union with God, feeling God's presence within and around us, and resonating the Truth so that others respond in kind with health and wholeness.

Spiritual Roots of Science of Mind

In this class I have felt seen, affirmed, challenged and guided. The readings were deep and challenging. It was taught by Reverend Ruth Barnhart whom I like very much. Our class discussions were helpful to put the readings into the context of our own lives. There are specific ideas from each author that have been useful to me.

Useful thoughts from Ralph Waldo Emerson:

- We experience the Infinite only to the degree that It expresses Itself through us, becoming to us that which we believe it to be.
- Prayer is the contemplation of facts from the highest point of view.
- "Bloated Nothingness" is the false evaluation which we place upon things.
- Spirituality is the atmosphere of God's Presence, Goodness, Truth and Beauty.
- We live in the eternal now.
- Our faith comes in glimpses and our vices are habitual.

Useful thoughts from Thomas Troward:

- A seed thought – an idea or concept that is focused on every day and I observe how I see the Divine moving it along in my life.
- The distinctive power of Spirit is thought, the distinctive power of Matter is form.
- The subjective mind is the organ of the Absolute and the objective mind is the organ of the Relative.
- We understand our projections by seeing what dynamics keep appearing on our lives.
- We should not limit our expectations of the future c
- There is Primary Cause, subjective and unconscious mind, and Secondary Cause, consciousness, intellectual mind, time and space.

- Form a clear concept in the objective mind of the idea we wish to convey to the subjective mind.
- The basis of all healing is a change in belief.
- The Universal Mind is always to us exactly what we believe it to be.

Useful thoughts from Emma Curtis Hopkins:

- God is omnipotent, omnipresent, and omniscient.
- In God I live and move and have my being.
- The I AM works through me to will and to do that which ought to be done by me.
- Mind will demonstrate as much greatness as it has courage to stand by its intention.
- I am to keep the words of truth going within me continuously.
- I must give up guilt (belief in personal sin or wrongdoing) and blame (the belief in sin or wrongdoing of others).
- I pronounce myself as a spiritual being with spiritual powers to heal.

Thanksgiving

It is Thanksgiving. This is a special day in America, a national holiday, where we gather together as families to eat turkey, dressing, cranberry sauce, and pumpkin pie to celebrate the first meal between the settlers and Indians, supposedly. It is a "family" holiday and can bring up a lot of feelings for most people.

This year we found out late that both caregivers were taking off the week to be with their families. That meant that Eric would go up to take care of Becky for five days. I was not too thrilled about that. We discussed it and agreed that he would come back on Friday after the Thursday Thanksgiving to give us a day together. That felt o.k. to both of us.

Last night I decided to go to the choir celebration at the Center for Spiritual Living. It was wonderful, very uplifting. The other day as I was on my walk, I noticed two cars that are frequently parked along my route that probably contain homeless men. They are allowed to stay the night in the park with a pass obtained upon entrance to the park. I decided to get a box lunch from Kentucky Fried Chicken for each one and drop it off which I did and it was great fun. I met on man, Pete, and his cat. The other did not leave his van to get the food so I left if on his windshield. It felt good to think of others. I also heard from my sponsor and sponsees.

I am feeling very thankful at this moment. I got an email from the wife of the film produced in France who wants to turn my book into a film, saying how much she liked my new video by Carol O'Dell on my website. She said it made her cry. It made me cry also. Although I wrote it, it was delivered with such sensitivity and the story is so dear that it made me cry. How blessed I am to have lived this experience!

A Dinner Party

My last class at the Center for Spiritual Living has ended and, as usual, I find myself feeling a bit restless. I have decided to have a dinner party, which I oftentimes do in between classes. I plan to invite around six people which makes eight with Eric and I, a nice size. I think everyone will enjoy each other's company as most do not yet know each other.

I enjoy having dinner parties. It was a bit difficult for me at first when I became sober but I have found that good discussions, sparkling cyder and delicious food make for a fun evening for me. I plan to use Leslie's mother's china from France which is white with a gold ring around it which will be festive for the holidays. Over the years I have collected lots of china, silver place settings, table cloths and cloth napkins, crystal wine glasses and serving dishes. The table always looks wonderful. This is how my mother used to set the dinner table for guests and for holidays so it feels comfortable for me. To my surprise, many have not had this experience. But most seem to enjoy the elegance and feel spoiled by having it.

I have the menu planned, a simple anti-pasta plate followed by lasagna with a green salad and garlic French bread then sorbet and chocolates for dessert. I love to cook and my lasagna always gest rave reviews. I have found the most awkward part of the evening can be after dessert. What to do or talk about? Instead of brandy, I propose a topic for discussion. At the last dinner party, the topic was "a favorite book," which I thought would be easy because I love to read. However, I discovered some at the dinner did not enjoy reading so it was difficult for them to answer. This time it will be "to recall a few of the most wonderful moments of the past year." That should end it all on an upbeat note. I'll write more about this after the event.

I have invited the guests and am awaiting the rsvp's. I look forward to the event in two weeks on a Sunday evening at 6:00 p.m.

A Christmas Tree

Eric came home unannounced this afternoon with a Christmas Tree. We had not discussed buying one, it just showed up along with two wreaths, 50 feet of garland for the outside porch railings, and honey covered peanuts. He was delighted. I was not.

This is just another example of him showing up with stuff for our home without talking to me about it. I feel crowded out of my own home. He insisted it would fit into the living room and after moving all of the furniture around, it did.

While he was doing this, I was feeling claustrophobic and a knot was forming in my stomach. I felt like there was not an inch of space left anymore for me in my own home, that he has totally taken over. I burst into tears. What seemed to him to be a wonderful festive activity felt like a violation to me. We tried to talk about it but will need to pick it up with the therapist tomorrow.

Leslie, my wife and life partner of twenty years died on December 27 five years ago. Each Christmas has been a dreaded time for me. I try to get through the holidays with as little disruption to my normal routine as possible. For me it is a painful time and this was exasperated by having stuff brought into my home further invading my space. Eric said he is dealing with his feelings of loss by buying things, stuffing down his feelings, and trying to enjoy the holidays. I feel like emotionally disconnecting from the whole thing. We couldn't be farther apart in our reactions.

Instead of feeling uplifted I feel thrust into my grief for Leslie. I feel a sense of deep loss. Five years ago, Leslie was on her death bed upstairs hanging onto life. She died at 3:00 a.m. on December 27, 2014. I was sleeping next to her and woke up when she had her last breath. It was a terrible time for me.

I was trying to let in the holiday spirit and even lighted a pine scented candle last night that Eric had bought for me trying to get into the spirit of things. Now the deep grief has surfaced again. I feel raw. Tears are streaming down my face. The grief is back full force. I haven't felt this bad since two Christmases ago when Amy, my sponsor, comforted me. I am not being comforted. I am being confronted with her loss. The thought of hanging up the Christmas ornaments, hand painted glass ones from Germany that I bought for her one each year, just makes me feel her loss more. I feel deep grief that hurts my heart.

Eric keeps repeating how much he loves this season and wants to celebrate. He keeps hanging up ornaments around the house. I don't know what to do. I want to go for a walk but it is late and dark and cold outside.

I can only wait for relief to come. I guess this is part of my healing process.

We saw our therapist, Peter, and he pointed out that right now I need stability in my life. I need for nothing to change.

A Tree Fell

Last night in the 50 mile an hour winds and rain a pine tree in my front yard broke, fell, and tore down all cable lines to my home and my neighbor's home which in turn caught the edge of our gutters on the front of the house which in turn fell down onto the top of the carport. Thank God I just had the carport built or it would have totally damaged my Mercedes. I am so upset I cannot sleep.

This morning at 9:00 a.m. the neighbor woke me up yelling at me about how outraged she was by my neglect of the tree and what an immense inconvenience it is to her to be without her internet access for four days. I have been trying to get the tree taken down for the last three weeks. I had PG&E out but their said it wasn't touching their wires so it was the landlord's problem. I had my landscaper out who said he would send me a quote. Well it was not taken care of in time and now we have this mess.

I have contacted the appropriate authorities to fix the lines and file a homeowner's claim for the damages. So, things will get taken care of in time. I wrote my neighbor an apology card enclosing $250.00 cash to compensate for her inconvenience which made her feel better.

But what has surfaced louder than anything is the fact that five years ago on December 27, 2014 my life partner and wife of twenty years Leslie died of cancer. I had been barely holding onto my center but with all of the turmoil of late the grief had come crashing into my consciousness. I just went to the service at the Center for Spiritual Living and cried all of the way through it. I went to a prayer treatment afterward and then saw my instructor Rev. Ruth who comforted me and reminded me that grief comes in waves and that I need to be gentle with myself, that it will pass. That is the only thing that makes sense right now: that I am in deep grief once again and just need to get through it as best as I can and be gentle with myself in the process. I feel exhausted from crying and handling problems in my life and with Eric's mother who has Alzheimer's. I have no energy to do anything so will go to bed to rest. lift my spirits.

I will log onto the CSL website to sign up for a new class in January which will lift my spirits. Then I will take a nap.

I awoke feeling rested and in touch with my very tender heart. I decided to rent and watch the movie Harold and Maude. Harold represents the emptiness that is felt by a sensitive young man who is surrounded by a superficial reality. He tries desperately to communicate to his mother his sense of hopelessness by staging fake suicides, which she ignores and deals with in inappropriate ways. Maude represents the zest for life that someone close to death can understand. It is about real issues that I understand. I like it.

I know part of my sorrow is that Eric is gone so much at his mom's. He has spent eight of the last twelve days up there, is up there now, and will spend four of the next seven days up there. I hope we can get her placed into a home in the new year.

A Dream

I just awoke from a very deep sleep and a dream. In my dream I was back in Chico living in the little house that my parents bought for me to live in while I was doing my Bachelor's and Master's work. I was not in the home but looking behind it at the white garage of the owner of the larger property I was a part of. They were a quiet retired couple. I lived in the country. I was happy there. In fact, it was one of the happiest times of my life, living alone, going to school, studying Ju Jitsu and working at Tower Records. In my dream I thought: "why did I even leave? I would have been happy there. Why didn't I just stay there?" But it was not enough at the time. For some reason I have kept pushing myself onward toward more. Why is that? More is not the answer.

In Chico I had very little money. I remember I could not afford tomatoes at the store. I lived on $250.00 a month including rent to my parents. Still I was happy. I was in touch with myself. I was putting myself through college on a Pell Grant, a scholarship, and working the six to midnight shift at Tower Records. Chico is in the valley in California which means that the summers are hot, in the 100's. I fondly remember bicycling home after work on warm summer evenings. I felt safe and content bicycling through the town at night. I was at peace.

Now I find myself wanting to simplify and go inward. I am looking forward to my next class at the Center for Spiritual Living on daily spirituality. I will be reading Journey of Awakening: A Meditator's Guidebook by Ram Dass and Can We Talk to God? by Ernest Holmes. I have already ordered them so I can start reading now. I feel adrift when I am not in a class at the Center. I seem to be happiest now again living simply, going inward.

I have been a seeker. I am seeking to know and experience life. Where does this come from? I am always pushing. I awake each morning, get out of bed, grab a protein bar and drive to the park to walk five miles around the lake.

I do this every day knowing that if I don't, I will be disappointed with myself for not going and will probably not sleep well that night either. I seem to be "programmed" to push myself!

The Dinner Party

We had the dinner party and it was the best one I have ever had. It was such a delightful combination of people who all got along so well together. I have never laughed so much. Most were in recovery and the last person did not mind that we had sparkling cider instead of wine (some people do and I don't invite them over now, maybe later). One guest is a musician and when he saw my 1935 restored Chickering Baby Grand piano he just had to play it much to all of our entertainment. On the table in the living room I had a Christmas orchid that had just bloomed. It was gorgeous and very special. It only blooms every other year.

At the end of the dinner I asked each person to share some favorite memories from 2019. What a wonderful way to get people to open their hearts to one another! We all found out things about each other that we had not known before.

I realized that this year I have been able to form new friendships that are very dear to me and to Eric. What a gift that is in life! I had been feeling a lack of friends and recall talking about it to Frances in therapy. Thanks to my dinner parties, going to the Center for Spiritual Living, and recovery we have found people we have a lot in common with. Everyone expressed appreciation for my dinner parties which surprised me. My mother taught me how to be a good hostess and I so appreciate that side of myself. It takes about two weeks for me to plan and execute a dinner party. I prepare the food and set the table the day before so I can enjoy the beauty of the fine china, silver and crystal that I have. It is a joy to look at and everyone always comments on it. It is a way for me to spoil my friends for an evening.

I usually thrown a dinner party between my classes at the Center for Spiritual Living. During my ten-week classes I am so busy with homework and class that I do not have the time and energy to do it. But when the class ends, I seem to always feel a loss and throwing a dinner party is just the thing to raise my spirits.

What a blessing that I can now relax while doing so. I used to have so much social anxiety that I drank a lot. Now I feel comfortable with myself and others and able to just stay in the moment and experience it all unfolding. I have given up my need to control which feel so much better!

Christmas

Today is Christmas. I have had the most wonderful two days.

Last night, Christmas Eve, we went to the Candle Lighting Service at the Center for Spiritual Living. It was just what I had hoped it would be and more. As a child we always went to the Candle Light Service at the Lutheran Church after a delicious Swedish dinner prepared by my mom. This year, there was a chorus and orchestra of about 50 people. It sounded very professional and moving. We started by singing some Christmas carols then the orchestra and chorus took over. There was a sermon by Rev. Edward. He discussed the many holy days that occur at this time of year: the lighting of the lamps of the Menorah, a Jewish tradition; winter solstice; and of course, the birth of Jesus in the Christian tradition. All of these celebrate the coming of the light after the darkness of the longest day of the year. They also celebrate the Divine Love that is present and available in each moment. At the end of the service each person was invited to come up front and light a candle from the Center Candle. As we did this, we were to reflect of what we were lighting our candle for. I lite mine in honor of brining the Divine Love into my heart more fully in the coming year. The entire service was so moving that I cried throughout. The presence of the Divine was palpable. My heart was opened with the joy of receiving it. Then we all sang Silent Night and Joy to the World.

Today we went to the early morning service. We had Spiritual Mind Treatments and reflections on the reality of the Divine Loving Presence available to us each moment. We reflected on, as it saying in A Course in Miracles, that each of us is either extending love or calling for it. How hard it is to remember this when the other person is hiding their love behind layers of hurt, pain, and suffering and lashing out at us in pain. Their call for love often feels like an attack, as it may be. However, our task is to realize that and remember the tender loving soul beneath all of the pain. We sang Christmas Carols and greeted one another.

What a blessing it is to be able to gather and have these rituals. They are moving and very powerful. Not everyone in the world is allowed to do this. Yet they find their own secret ways to worship. It is in our nature to remember and long for the Light in the Darkness. May I remember this all year long!

My Support System

I have come to realize that I have a support system that keeps me balanced, feeling loved and loving, and spiritually nourished. Most important, upon awakening I turn my will and life over to God. This reestablishes the new basis of my reality – trusting in and resting in my Higher Power each moment of the day. Next, I go for my five mile walk around the lake. Here I routinely see friends I have come to know who have the same habit. We don't usually stop to talk but just say "hi" in a friendly sort of way. I feel connected to others.

Then I go to breakfast at a restaurant in town that is frequented by locals. It is owned by an extended Mexican family and it feels like I have become one of them. They ask where Eric, my husband, is if not along, which has been quite a lot lately. Due to problems with caregivers for his mom taking off time for the holidays he has only been home five days this month, so I am getting used to him being gone. It has been good for me to get in touch with myself again. I find I am doing more spiritual reading and meditation with him gone. I plan to continue this practice and am starting a new class on medication soon.

I come home from breakfast and work on this book, answer emails about my first book and take care of things. I try to find time to watch the PBS Newshour each day to keep up on current events even though there seems to be so much turmoil in the world.

In the evenings I often go to a recovery meeting or to a class at the Center for Spiritual Living. I find emotional support there from many new friends. I also offer support to newcomers remembering well my fears and trepidation when first walking through those doors.

Tonight, I have been asked to share at a recovery meeting my experience, strength and hope. I look forward to this opportunity. I have changed so much for the better and love life now when before I was suicidal. I received an email from a friend who is not in recovery saying that psychotherapy and antidepressants are an answer to alcoholism.

wrote back saying that had not worked for me and I would not go back to drinking for anything. It shocked me that he would suggest it. I think he is considering it for himself as he is in recovery and smokes marijuana a lot which is just escaping from reality. It made me realize how joyful I am about this new life. For me, the spiritual path is my answer. I get help from suggestions and sharing from others as well as from books and classes. I now feel in the presence must of the time and when I am out of it, it is obvious by my anxiety and emotional suffering. I try to get back to center, as I call it, as soon as possible.

No one could have explained to me in my darkest hours the joyful path that would unfold for me. I was convinced I was through having anything to offer to this world when I walked into recovery. That gift of desperation facilitated my willingness to do all that was suggested to me to turn away from alcohol and learn a new way of living. Today is full of hope and promise. When the structure of my previous life fell away (retired from career; my wife of twenty years, Leslie, died and I was swallowed up in grief and sadness; the house was nearly destroyed by a water heater leak and had to be rebuilt from the inside out...) I realized I had nothing to stand on. I turned to alcohol which is not my friend but rather took me down deeper and deeper into despair.

I think this is why I can so appreciate every little piece of my day which gives me meaning today. Each part is a unique gift from the universe. I am so grateful and would not change it for the world. I am expecting more goodness and service to unfold each day. I belong and am a part of the solution not the problem. I have found that I am a spiritual being having a physical experience. I am no longer defined by my externals. I am defined by my internal walk with the Divine. This is a priceless gift!

The New Year

A New Year has begun. Some people set goals for themselves in the beginning of a new year. They usually do not come true. Why is this? I think it is because they create a picture of the future based upon ideals about themselves that are not yet real. They imagine a new personality or way of coping with life as if that can magically happen. I would like to suggest another approach: using intention. Goals are in the future, while intentions are present tense.

It is so important that we train our minds to feed them with the thoughts we want to guide our lives. The most fruitful way to do that is by accepting into our lives that which we want to attract. In other words, instead of saying "I will have friends" you say to yourself "I have friends." That simple switch moves the focus from something that will be attained in the future (when I will be happy, fulfilled, et cetera) to the present. The task then becomes to notice and appreciate the friends that are in your life and are coming into your life.

I did this a year ago. I was aware that I had changed so much that my old friends, except a few, no longer seemed to share my current interests and way of seeing the world and I wanted to create a new network of friends, a new social fabric for myself. I started asking myself to notice when I met someone if I felt a sense of connection with them. If so, I started to pursue conversations with them. This included people in recovery meetings, at my church, during my walks around the lake each morning. Then I took the big step of inviting them to my home for small dinner parties which can allow for further deepening of connection and mutual understanding. This took a lot of courage on my part. I was still unfamiliar with entertaining without alcohol being involved. Still I prepared the menu and reminded myself that the purpose of the event was to simply enjoy new people in my life; that I could relax and let the event unfold. I served sparkling cider instead of wine and found that the evenings went quite well. I've added peaceful mediation music quietly going on in the background which helps me to relax and I believe helps my guests relax as well. The conversation does indeed carry the evening and we all have a great time.

Intention involves mentally stating what we want to manifest in our lives and then noticing when these things show up and then building on that, following the path. This means being in the present moment, paying attention and responding. It also involves trust rather than force. I don't force my will upon myself and others, I listen with my intuition to the guidance that I receive. It is getting into the flow of life rather than forcing it to my will.

Divine Love

God is love. All religions teach this. But what kind of love is it? I think I have an idea. When I was sixteen years old getting ready for a Modern Dance Concert at my High School, my mother was sewing some fabric onto my tights and leotard in the atrium in our home. It was a hot Saturday afternoon. I fainted and hit my head on a rock. What I experienced was my body floating above my physical body, on my back with my feet first. It was dark all around me but I wasn't scared. I was rather curious. I saw a speck of light way ahead and started floating toward it. As I got closer to the light, I felt an unconditional love I had never known on this earth. I knew I was returning home and wanted to stay there. There were beings of light around me. I was thinking about some bad behaviors in my life and I felt them reassure me that I had done nothing wrong, rather, that they understood what I was trying to do and understood and then encouraged me to love myself. I then heard my mother and sister calling me and awoke on the living room couch surrounded by them and the family doctor. I had been out about a half hour.

I never told anyone about this experience realizing that it was unusual, other worldly. Years later when I was working at Tower Books and Records I saw the book Near Death Experiences by Raymond Moody. I read it and realized that was what I had experienced. This was reassuring.

I believe that this is Divine Love. I experience it when I pray to turn my will and life over to my Higher Power. I experienced it when I was at the Candlelight Service this year and it made me cry. It is such a sweetness. It fills my heart.

I think I need to meditate on this sweetness. I need to practice devotion to fill my heart and increase my awareness of this goodness. I also need to apply it to myself and others, to not judge. This can be very challenging. I am working on it.

Spiritual Mind Treatment To Release Worry

One of the changes I have noticed in my life is how I deal with troubling situations. When I realize I have confusion or worry about a situation or person, I try to identify the God quality of the solution and do a Spiritual Mind Treatment for it. For example, recently I have been concerned about the direction for this book: how to proceed, which publisher to go with, who to contact for help. I immediately did a Treatment for my confusion.

Purpose: Clarity about how to proceed with publishing this book.

Recognition: Spirit is present now. It is the Source of all creation: the beauty of the forests, the majesty of the oceans, the clouds, the untold universes that swirl around in perfect orbit. This Source holds and sustains all that exists.

Unification: I am an individualized expression of the Divine. In God I live and move and have my being. I am guided and led to all that I need in life. I am united with this Spirit.

Realization: I know that I have clarity about how to proceed with the publishing of this manuscript. I am guided by the Divine Spirit to fulfill my work on this earth. I am a servant of the Divine. I rest and move and have my being in Source. I am able to discern the direction for my book: who to talk to about it, how to proceed. I release all worry. I claim clarity and peace.

Thanksgiving: I know that the Law of Life has acted upon my words and it is already done. I give thanks for the reality of Spirit in my life. I am blessed.

Release: I simply let go, get God, and rest assured that all is well. And so it is.

Then I let go and go about my day. I am sensitive to the leading of Spirit in my life. Sunday in service I was led to ask Rev. Edward Viljoen about my publishing questions. He is a published author and spiritual guide so I thought he would be a good person to ask. He did give me feedback which was useful and a website for more guidance. I received a call from an agent wanting to represent me so I sent that person this draft and a synopsis of the book. I now rest in the assurance that all is unfolding as it should.

This shift from worry to Spiritual Mind Treatment has been profound. I find that instead of focusing on a problem I am switching my attention to the solution to that problem and to God. It makes my life my easier. I feel more peace.

Spiritual Mind Treatment for Forgiveness

I am learning in my class Treatment and Meditation how to do affirmative prayer treatment for others. This week the assignment was to do a treatment for a prayer partner. In class she discussed with me how her anger was keeping her down spiritually, that she was learning to forgive and it was setting her free. I wrote a treatment for her to continue in this direction.

Purpose: For release anger and forgiveness.

Recognition: There is One Divine Presence. It is Love. It is in all things seen and unseen. It is in the stars and planets displayed in the night sky. It is in the plants, trees, animals, fish, majestic mountains, awesome oceans. It is ever present, all powerful and all knowing.

Unification: I am connected to this Presence. It flows through me as me in every moment. As this is true for me it is true for my prayer partner. She is an individualized expression of the Divine, perfect and whole.

Realization: I speak my word for her. I declare that she releases all anger and judgement of herself and others. She naturally lets go of these feelings and accepts forgiveness in her heart. She feels a healing in her heart and soul for all perceived wrongs of the past. She lets them go and lets in Light, Love, and Wholeness. She is free from the past. She lives in the present moment aware of God's Presence in herself and others. She is healed.

Thanksgiving: For this shift in consciousness I give thanks. I realize it has already happened. It is done.

Release: So I simply let it go.

And so it is.

Moss and Ferns

I went for my morning walk around the lake today. I had not been there for four days due to rain and commitments to recovery and the Center for Spiritual Learning.

I was struck by the beauty of the scenery. The rain had prompted a gorgeous layer of moss to grow on the trees and forest floor. Small ferns had sprung up among the dried leaves and moss. The forest looked alive and magical.

Geese were calling loudly announcing themselves. It is mating season. They are finding mates, establishing territory and making nests. In April and May, the fruits of their union will burst forth. Flocks of yellow puff balls will appear following around their mother and pecking at the grass. I will watch as they grow during the Fall.

How wonderous to observe nature, to notice it where before I had just walked by absorbed in my thoughts. I've come to realize my walks are a meditation. They are a time to notice nature and calm my active mind. I stop half way through the walk at a bench I call the "serenity bench." The scene is always the same: the lake so peaceful and serene with clouds and ducks, surrounding trees reflected in the lake like a mirror. Today there were two mud hens diving down and popping up a few minutes later ten or twenty feet away.

I was blessed to grow up on a lake. I had many days and hours to explore nature. It was in Oregon which is very wet and lush. The lake where I walk now reminds me of that time.

It's strange how my life had passed so quickly, at least, that is how it feels now. At the time though there were many hardships to endure and learn from.

I am so thankful for this phase of my life. I have time to reflect and enjoy life, to notice and help others. I enjoyed that part of teaching college students, helping them with their personal struggles. I get to do that now with my sponsees and in treating for others from the Center for Spiritual Living. It feels good to give. I feel like the moss and ferns: so full of life that I have some to give away. There is an abundance of energy and grace.

I saw one tree blooming. It had little white flowers on it that looked like little lanterns, about thirty in a bunch throughout the tree branches. It looked like nature had decorated the tree with light.

I feel blessed, and peaceful.

Thursdays

Thursdays are my favorite day of the week. It is the day that Eric and I take off for ourselves to be together. In the early afternoons we leave to drive up the coast. The highway is windy and goes along the beautiful Pacific Ocean. I love to drive along the twisty roads driving as fast as I can in my car which handles so well and hugs the road on every turn. I manage to stay in the right lane most of the time but sometimes drift over to the wrong side of the road for a brief moment.

It takes a half hour to get from our home to the coast. We pass over gorgeous rolling hills with fields of green grass, ranches with cows and sheep, old windmills and picturesque farm houses. Then we dip down to the ocean, smell the salty air, and see the first waves rolling in. It is at this point that I always think about the many Thursday afternoons for thirty years that I sat behind a desk looking at a computer screen doing emails, analyzing data and writing reports. I then feel the freedom of the open road ahead and a sense of adventure with what lies ahead: three hours of open road, the ocean to my left as we head up North to a small town where we stop for dinner. During dinner we sit and look at the ocean, the fishing boats coming in from a day's catch, the seals swimming in the harbor, sea gulls flying by, the sun setting into the bay.

Driving back Eric drives and I get to look at the scenery. I notice the large ranches with cows and sheep and horses wandering freely on the hillsides. Along the road are redwoods hundreds of years old stretching up seventy feet high into the air. Moss and ferns frame the highway. Deer, foxes, skunks and mice run across the road. Sometimes we see large hawks on the telephone wires peering down at us. Tonight, there was a half-moon shining on the ocean illuminating the waves and the cliffs below.

Most of the time we have the radio on. We are in the moment enjoying the pleasure of free time together. We listen to a satellite station that plays music from the '70s. We sing along to Into the Mystic by Van Morrison, You've Got a Friend by Carole King and other favorites by the Doobie Brothers, James Taylor, Gordon Lightfoot, the Rolling Stones and many others. Our minds drift and we share thoughts we've had during the week, what has moved us, what we are concerned with, the joys and sorrows.

It is time apart from all worries and concerns of daily life. There is no cell phone service so we are not interrupted. I feel just in the present moment, aware of the curve in the road, the clouds in the sky, the ocean waves below. It renews me. I feel peace and gratitude. I am blessed.

Spiritual Mind Treatment

Purpose: For my prayer partner to identify her feelings, journal about them, and be true to herself in thought and action.

Recognition: One Spirit is present now. It flows in and through all that exists, all that is manifest and unmanifest. It has always been, is present now, and will always be. It is a force for Good. It is a force for fulfillment, clarity, consciousness and unification. It is all knowing, always providing guidance and lighting the path before us. It is for us. It has all power. There is no lack in Spirit.

Unification: I am one with the awesome force. It is my source, my expression, my life. I consciously unite with the Power for Good in all my actions and thoughts. And as this is so for me it is so for her.

Realization: She feels the welling up of feelings that guide her in her life to understand life's circumstances and make wise choices for herself. She trusts this Spirit, has faith in its ever-present guidance, trusts and follows her feelings. She takes time daily to turn inward and discern her feelings, to notice her reactions to life, to honor her inner guidance. She trusts and follows this inner knowing, writes about it daily in her journal, and applies these new insights into her life. She is creating a new life path for herself based upon self-knowledge, self-trust, and self-regard.

Thanksgiving: For this awareness in her, for her desire to change and move her life in this new direction, I give thanks for I know it has already taken place in Spirit. The Law has acted upon new feelings and insights and she rests in peace as a life of harmony for her unfolds.

Release: Knowing that the Word has been spoken and the Law has acted upon it, I rest in complete confidence that it is done. I release this Prayer and let God.

Purpose: For Eric to know that his sister's surgery will go well, that she will live through it.

Recognition: The is One Infinite Divine Love at the very center and through all that exists. This Power and Intelligence created this magnificent world and the expansion of the universes that stretch beyond our comprehension.

Unification: This same wisdom flows through us, guiding and nurturing us at every moment. I know that I am united with this force, this intelligence, it has made me and breathes me every second of my life. It continues after the death of this physical body. I am a Spirit having a human experience. And as this is true for me it is true for Eric and her. In God we live and move and have our being. There is no where we can go where God is not present, holding us in Its Loving Embrace.

Realization: I claim for Eric a new emergence of this knowledge, a peace and tranquility of the Loving Guidance that lights his way every second of every day. Eric feels a certainty in his mind and heart and body that God is here with him and with her. In the operating room, God is. In the preparation, in every action during the surgery, in every moment of the recovery, God is present. We live and move and have out being in God, in Goodness, in Oneness, in Peace and Wholeness. Our healthy bodies reflect this fact. Our healing reflects this fact. I know that she is increasing in awareness of her Divine Self through this illness. The process is healing her spirit, mind, emotions and body.

Thanksgiving: I give thanks for the completeness of this Treatment. I know the words have been placed into the hands of the Divine Healer and they are being acted upon now and in the future.

Release: All is done so I simply let go and let God.

Spiritual Mind Treatment for Rose

Purpose: For me for the gift that I am in this life.

Recognition: There is One Creative Divine Intelligence that is the Source of all that exists, all that has been and all that will be. That One is God. That Source is unconditional love. It is a force for our Good. It says "yes" to all our thoughts. It creates.

Unification: I am one with this Source. It is the origin of my life ever flowing through me as I cocreate with it to a demonstration of my understanding of it. My thoughts create my body and life experience through God. God is in, around, and through me.

Realization: I realize that I am a unique creation of the Divine. I have a Divine purpose in being on this earth at this time in history. I have unique ways of expressing Good in the world. God moves through me. I am God's voice, God's touch, God's thoughts, God's expression in my writing and speech. Divine Intuition guides me at all times to do that which I am to do and be. I relax into the Love of God and feel serenity and peace, the serenity of my soul.

Thanksgiving: For this recognition I give thanks. For this awareness I am overfilled with gratitude for the reality of Divine Expression through and as me. I thank God for this truth.

Release: Having said my word I know the Law of Life is giving it expression now and in the future. I simply release and let go and let God. And so it is.

What is Spiritual Mind Treatment?

The world's great religions agree that there is one creative intelligence that underlies all reality. It is called many different names: God, Allah, Yahweh, Jehovah, First Cause, Chi, Qi, Adonai, Hashem, Krishna, Buddha nature, Tao, the I AM. God is ever present, all knowing, and all powerful. It is power, beauty, light, love, benevolence, kindness, forgiveness, peace, and serenity. It is ever drawing us closer to Itself.

Ernest Holmes distilled this understanding into the Science of Mind philosophy. He states that in the macrocosm the Word, or First Cause, is the origin of all that has ever existed or will exist. It is eternal. Thought proceeds manifestation. In the microcosm humans create their life experiences by their thoughts conscious and unconscious. Most of our deepest thoughts about ourselves come from our family and society and are unconscious. We accept on some level that we are not good enough; that we are inferior because of the color of our skin, our gender, our sexual orientation, our disabilities...that we are not worthy. These thought forms are creating our existence oftentimes beyond our awareness. Therefore, it is essential that we bring to consciousness our assumptions about life and ourselves.

Ernest Holmes and others teach that we can heal ourselves and others through the use of Affirmative Prayer called Spiritual Mind Treatment. In this process the practitioner claims for themselves and the other, the reality of their Divine Existence devoid of illness or lack of any kind.

Emmet Fox in his book The Sermon on the Mount states that Jesus taught spiritually or metaphysically. Fox states that serenity is tranquility of the soul. "To pray scientifically means to affirm that God is helping us, that temptation has no power against us, and to constantly claim that our own real nature is spiritual and perfect (p. 55). "

In The Lord's Prayer Jesus teaches us to accept each day our daily bread. We are to expect that God will provide us fully with everything we need. "Bread does not merely mean food but all that that we require for a healthy, happy, free, and harmonious life. This includes food, clothing, shelter, means to travel, books, and so on; above all, we require freedom" (Fox, p. 162). We are free to choose to accept the Divine Goodness or rely on our own self for supply.

Surrender is required in order to experience God's perfect Grace. Most us of surrender a little bit at a time. We may pray in the morning, meditate for a half hour, go to yoga class, and give thanks in the evening. We may experience peace and serenity at these times. Then we go back to our normal experiences of reality, strife, and anxiety. Emerson states "our faith comes in glimpses while our vices are perpetual." We are instructed by Jesus to pray without ceasing. We are to live in the Presence of God every moment of our lives.

For some surrender is complete and sudden. This opening is prompted by a feeling of desperation and the awareness that all that has had meaning in one's life before makes no sense, has led to failure, lack, and often suicidal thoughts. This awareness makes the person open to receive God's Grace and learn a new way of life. It is a gift of desperation that creates a willingness to release our hold on our life and let God take over. There is a shattering of the illusion of separateness and a restoration of the soul to its wholeness.

What are we to do when we experience lack? Joel Goldsmith in his book Practicing the Presence writes "The spiritual life reveals clearly that God's grace is our sufficiency in all things. We do not need anything in this world except His grace" (p. 83). When we experience lack we are to declare unreservedly that "Thy Grace is my sufficiency." Jesus teaches us "Seek ye first the kingdom of God and all else will be given unto you."

In Love Without End: Jesus Speaks by Glenda Green we read that Jesus told her that "at the center of your soul is the Sacred Heart. This is the point at which you are one with God. The heart sees infinity within and without…It can ascertain the origin of conditions and change them. The heart is your higher intelligence… Your mind is merely a servant and it behaves well if it is given positive impulses; it behaves very poorly if it is given negative impulses…It is from this power, within the center of your being that the entire script of your life is written. Live in your heart to either fulfill the script of your life or to rewrite it…The answers to healing your life will be found in the inner strength of your heart…Strengthen all of your positive emotions through daily gratitude and admirations. Disempower your negative emotions daily through forgiveness." (pp. 50-51).

Ernest Holmes in Can We Talk To God? writes "The secret of spiritual power is a consciousness of one's union with the whole and the availability of good" (p. 58). I think that in Spiritual Mind Treatment the power comes from dropping into our Sacred Heart and realizing our Divinity and the Divinity of those we treat. We then affirm the reality of the Goodness that comes from that Divine Inheritance. We place the mind in its proper place as a servant to our positive thoughts thereby stimulating the Law of Life to create that which we know to be true.

Show Me The Way

Show me the way. Show me the way.

Your love will light the way.

Show me the way. Show me the way.

Your love will light the way.

Nam..Nam..Nam..Namaste

Nam..Nam..Nam..Namaste

Namo..Namo..Namo..Namaste.

Show me the way. Show me the way.

Your love will light the way.

Show me the way. Show me the way.

Your love will light the way.

Nam..Nam..Nam..Namaste

Nam..Nam..Nam..Namaste

Namo..Namo..Namo..Namaste

Song by Karl Anthony.

www.ingramcontent.com/pod-product-compliance
Lightning Source LLC
Chambersburg PA
CBHW070050120526
44589CB00034B/1785